This bo

_____

_____

_____

Published by Andrew Wommack Ministries, Inc. Woodland Park, CO 80863

ISBN 13 TP:
ISBN 13 eBook:
ISBN 13 LP POD:
ISBN 13 HC POD:
Printed in the U.S.A.
2 3 4 5 6 7 8 / 25 24 23 22

Reflections of Intimacy

A one-month guided journal to capture your
reflections of intimacy with the Lord.

*Then you will call upon Me and go
and pray to Me, and I will listen to you.
And you will seek Me and find Me, when
you search for Me with all your heart.
I will be found by you, says the L*ORD.

Jeremiah 29:12–14a, *NKJV*

What I love about the Lord is that He is not hiding from us! He is actively looking to teach us, lead us, and answer prayer. Yet, that is why He invites us to *seek* Him!

We believe that as you use your time to seek Him, you will find all the good things He has already prepared for you.

Blessings,

Carrie Pickett

Assistant Vice President of Charis Bible College
and Andrew Wommack Ministries International Operations
Director of Charis Bible College Woodland Park

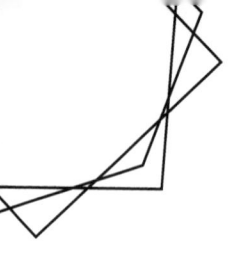

Matthew 6:33

*But seek first
the kingdom of God
and His righteousness,
and all these things
shall be added to you.*

(NKJV)

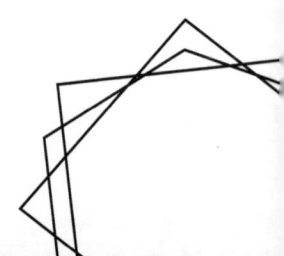

What is the Lord speaking to you about this scripture?

How will you apply this scripture to your life today?

Who will you share your reflection with today?

Deuteronomy 3:22

Do not be afraid of them;
the LORD your God
himself will fight for you.

(NIV)

What is the Lord speaking to you about this scripture?

How will you apply this scripture to your life today?

Who will you share your reflection with today?

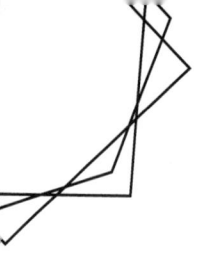

Psalm 100:4

Enter into His gates with thanksgiving, And into His courts with praise. Be thankful to Him, and bless His name.

(NKJV)

What is the Lord speaking to you about this scripture?

How will you apply this scripture to your life today?

Who will you share your reflection with today?

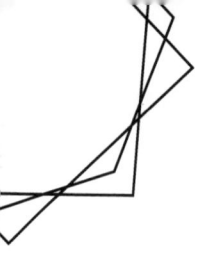

Matthew 11:28

Come to Me, all you who labor and are heavy laden, and I will give you rest.

(NKJV)

What is the Lord speaking to you about this scripture?

How will you apply this scripture to your life today?

Who will you share your reflection with today?

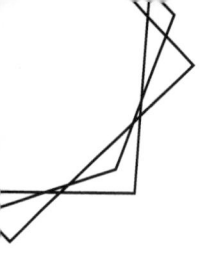

Isaiah 54:10

"For the mountains shall depart And the hills be removed, But My kindness shall not depart from you, Nor shall My covenant of peace be removed," Says the LORD, who has mercy on you.

(NKJV)

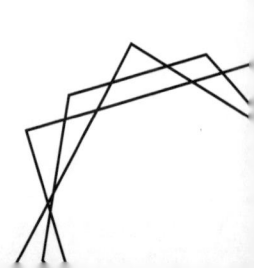

What is the Lord speaking to you about this scripture?

How will you apply this scripture to your life today?

Who will you share your reflection with today?

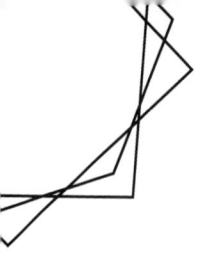

Psalm 119:105

Your word is a lamp
to my feet And
a light to my path.

(NKJV)

What is the Lord speaking to you about this scripture?

How will you apply this scripture to your life today?

Who will you share your reflection with today?

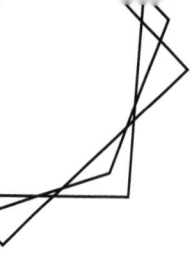

Nahum 1:7

The LORD is good, A stronghold in the day of trouble; And He knows those who trust in Him.

(NKJV)

What is the Lord speaking to you about this scripture?

How will you apply this scripture to your life today?

Who will you share your reflection with today?

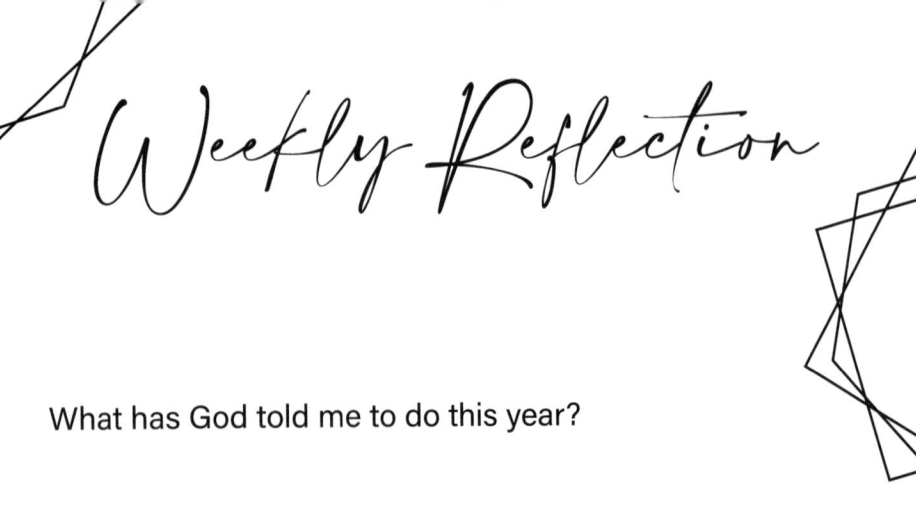

Weekly Reflection

What has God told me to do this year?

What is God saying now?

My next 3 steps to obey what God has said:

Gratitude

What did God do for me last week?

What am I believing God for this week?

I will show my gratitude to the Lord by:

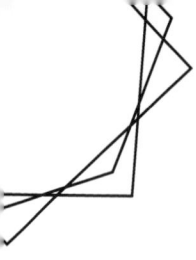

James 1:17

Every good gift and every perfect gift is from above, and comes down from the Father of lights, with whom there is no variation or shadow of turning.

(NKJV)

What is the Lord speaking to you about this scripture?

How will you apply this scripture to your life today?

Who will you share your reflection with today?

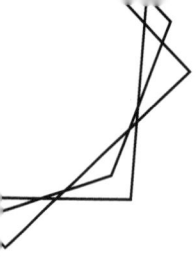

Psalm 23:6

Surely goodness and
mercy shall follow me
All the days of my life;
And I will dwell in the
house of the LORD Forever.

(NKJV)

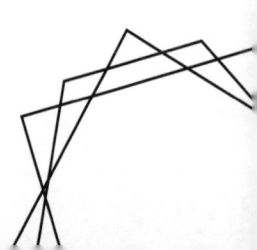

Reflection

What is the Lord speaking to you about this scripture?

How will you apply this scripture to your life today?

Who will you share your reflection with today?

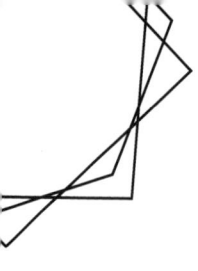

Ezekiel 36:26

I will give you a new heart and put a new spirit within you; I will take the heart of stone out of your flesh and give you a heart of flesh.

(NKJV)

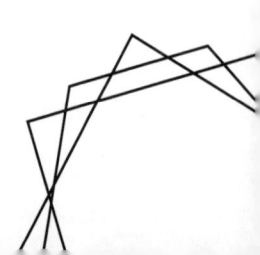

What is the Lord speaking to you about this scripture?

How will you apply this scripture to your life today?

Who will you share your reflection with today?

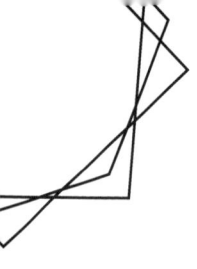

Jeremiah 31:25

For I have satiated the weary soul, and I have replenished every sorrowful soul.

(NKJV)

What is the Lord speaking to you about this scripture?

How will you apply this scripture to your life today?

Who will you share your reflection with today?

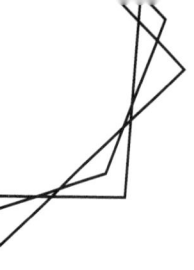

Revelation 3:20

Behold, I stand at the door and knock. If anyone hears My voice and opens the door, I will come in to him and dine with him, and he with Me.

(NKJV)

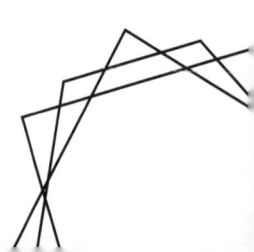

What is the Lord speaking to you about this scripture?

How will you apply this scripture to your life today?

Who will you share your reflection with today?

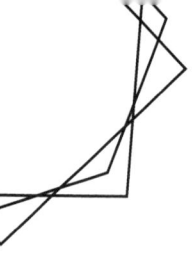

John 3:17

For God did not send His Son into the world to condemn the world, but that the world through Him might be saved.

(NKJV)

What is the Lord speaking to you about this scripture?

How will you apply this scripture to your life today?

Who will you share your reflection with today?

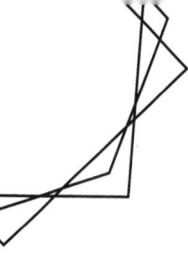

John 15:7

If you abide in Me,
and My words abide
in you, you will ask
what you desire, and
it shall be done for you.

(NKJV)

What is the Lord speaking to you about this scripture?

How will you apply this scripture to your life today?

Who will you share your reflection with today?

Weekly Reflection

What has God told me to do this year?

What is God saying now?

My next 3 steps to obey what God has said:

Gratitude

What did God do for me last week?

What am I believing God for this week?

I will show my gratitude to the Lord by:

Zephaniah 3:17

The LORD your God in your midst, The Mighty One, will save; He will rejoice over you with gladness, He will quiet you with His love, He will rejoice over you with singing.

(NKJV)

What is the Lord speaking to you about this scripture?

How will you apply this scripture to your life today?

Who will you share your reflection with today?

Romans 8:37–39

Yet in all these things we are more than conquerors through Him who loved us. For I am persuaded that neither death nor life, nor angels nor principalities nor powers, nor things present nor things to come, nor height nor depth, nor any other created thing, shall be able to separate us from the love of God which is in Christ Jesus our Lord.

(NKJV)

What is the Lord speaking to you about this scripture?

How will you apply this scripture to your life today?

Who will you share your reflection with today?

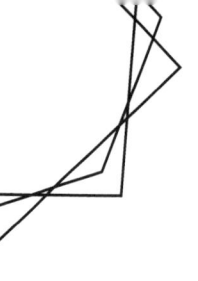

Isaiah 41:13

For I am the LORD your God who takes hold of your right hand and says to you, Do not fear; I will help you.

(NIV)

What is the Lord speaking to you about this scripture?

How will you apply this scripture to your life today?

Who will you share your reflection with today?

John 15:16

You have not chosen Me,
but I have chosen you
and I have appointed and
placed and purposefully
planted you, so that you
would go and bear fruit
and keep on bearing, and
that your fruit will
remain and be lasting, so
that whatever you ask of
the Father in My name
[as My representative]
He may give to you.

(AMP)

What is the Lord speaking to you about this scripture?

How will you apply this scripture to your life today?

Who will you share your reflection with today?

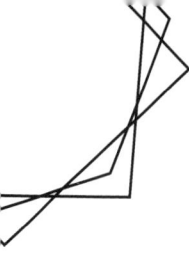

Psalm 27:14

Wait for and confidently
expect the LORD;
Be strong and let your
heart take courage; Yes,
wait for and confidently
expect the LORD.

(AMP)

What is the Lord speaking to you about this scripture?

How will you apply this scripture to your life today?

Who will you share your reflection with today?

John 16:33

I have told you these
things, so that in Me you
may have [perfect] peace.
In the world you have
tribulation and distress
and suffering, but
be courageous [be confident,
be undaunted, be filled
with joy]; I have
overcome the world.
[My conquest is accomplished,
My victory abiding.]

(AMP)

What is the Lord speaking to you about this scripture?

How will you apply this scripture to your life today?

Who will you share your reflection with today?

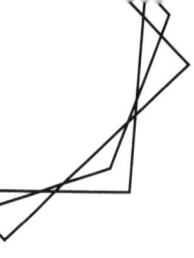

Proverbs 24:14

Know that [skillful and godly] wisdom is [so very good] for your life and soul: If you find wisdom, then there will be a future and a reward. And your hope and expectation will not be cut off.

(AMP)

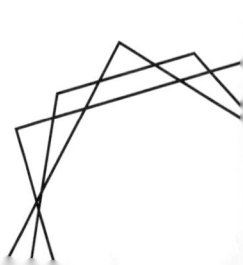

What is the Lord speaking to you about this scripture?

How will you apply this scripture to your life today?

Who will you share your reflection with today?

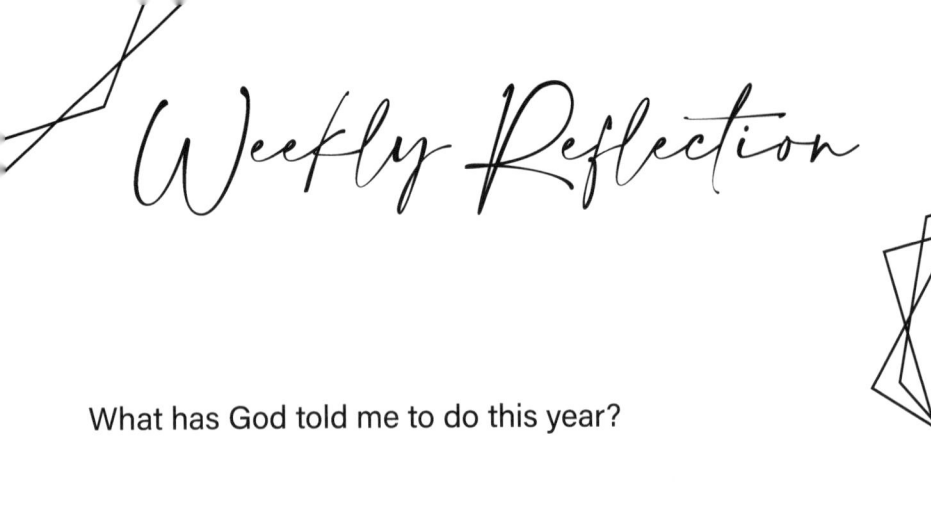

Weekly Reflection

What has God told me to do this year?

What is God saying now?

My next 3 steps to obey what God has said:

Gratitude

What did God do for me last week?

What am I believing God for this week?

I will show my gratitude to the Lord by:

2 Corinthians 4:18

So we look not at the things which are seen, but at the things which are unseen; for the things which are visible are temporal (just brief and fleeting) but the things which are invisible are everlasting and imperishable.

(AMP)

What is the Lord speaking to you about this scripture?

How will you apply this scripture to your life today?

Who will you share your reflection with today?

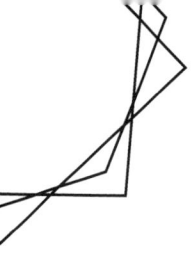

Judges 6:12

When the angel of the LORD appeared to Gideon, he said, "The LORD is with you, mighty warrior."

(NIV)

What is the Lord speaking to you about this scripture?

How will you apply this scripture to your life today?

Who will you share your reflection with today?

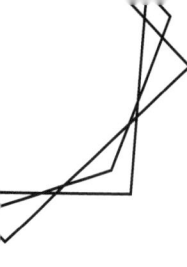

Isaiah 42:13

The LORD goes out like a mighty man, like a man of war he stirs up his zeal; he cries out, he shouts aloud, he shows himself mighty against his foes.

(ESV)

What is the Lord speaking to you about this scripture?

How will you apply this scripture to your life today?

Who will you share your reflection with today?

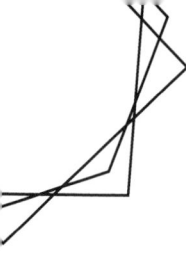

Proverbs 16:32

Whoever is slow to anger
is better than the mighty,
and he who rules his spirit
than he who takes a city.

(ESV)

What is the Lord speaking to you about this scripture?

How will you apply this scripture to your life today?

Who will you share your reflection with today?

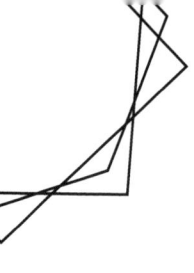

1 Chronicles 16:11

Seek the LORD and His strength; Seek His face continually [longing to be in His presence]

(AMP)

What is the Lord speaking to you about this scripture?

How will you apply this scripture to your life today?

Who will you share your reflection with today?

2 Timothy 1:9

For He delivered us and saved us and called us with a holy calling [a calling that leads to a consecrated life—a life set apart—a life of purpose] not because of our works [or because of any personal merit—we could do nothing to earn this] but because of His own purpose and grace [His amazing, undeserved favor] which was granted to us in Christ Jesus before the world began [eternal ages ago].

(AMP)

What is the Lord speaking to you about this scripture?

How will you apply this scripture to your life today?

Who will you share your reflection with today?

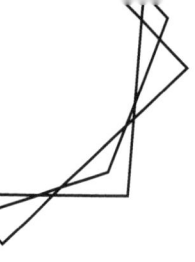

Numbers 23:19

God is not a man,
that He should lie,
Nor a son of man, that
He should repent. Has
He said, and will He
not do? Or has He
spoken, and will He
not make it good?

(NKJV)

What is the Lord speaking to you about this scripture?

How will you apply this scripture to your life today?

Who will you share your reflection with today?

Weekly Reflection

What has God told me to do this year?

What is God saying now?

My next 3 steps to obey what God has said:

Gratitude

What did God do for me last week?

What am I believing God for this week?

I will show my gratitude to the Lord by:

Reflections of Intimacy

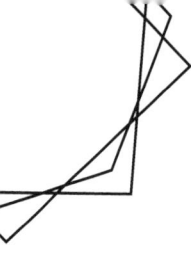

Isaiah 40:11

He will feed his flock
like a shepherd.
He will carry the
lambs in his arms,
holding them
close to his heart.

(NLT)

What is the Lord speaking to you about this scripture?

How will you apply this scripture to your life today?

Who will you share your reflection with today?

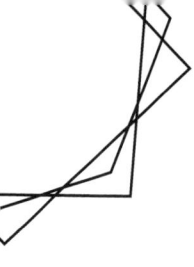

Psalm 27:10

Although my father and my mother have abandoned me, Yet the LORD will take me up [adopt me as His child].

(AMP)

What is the Lord speaking to you about this scripture?

How will you apply this scripture to your life today?

Who will you share your reflection with today?

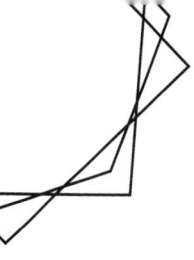

Psalm 73:26

My flesh and my heart may fail, but God is the strength of my heart and my portion forever.

(*NIV*)

What is the Lord speaking to you about this scripture?

How will you apply this scripture to your life today?

Who will you share your reflection with today?

Philippians 4:13

I can do all things through Christ who strengthens me.

(NKJV)

What is the Lord speaking to you about this scripture?

How will you apply this scripture to your life today?

Who will you share your reflection with today?

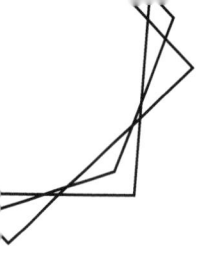

Proverbs 31:26

*She opens her mouth
with wisdom, and the
teaching of kindness
is on her tongue.*

(*ESV*)

What is the Lord speaking to you about this scripture?

How will you apply this scripture to your life today?

Who will you share your reflection with today?

Joshua 1:9

Have I not commanded you? Be strong and courageous. Do not be frightened, and do not be dismayed, for the LORD your God is with you wherever you go.

(ESV)

What is the Lord speaking to you about this scripture?

How will you apply this scripture to your life today?

Who will you share your reflection with today?

Jeremiah 29:11

"For I know the plans I have for you," declares the LORD, "plans to prosper you and not to harm you, plans to give you hope and a future."

(NIV)

What is the Lord speaking to you about this scripture?

How will you apply this scripture to your life today?

Who will you share your reflection with today?

Weekly Reflection

What has God told me to do this year?

What is God saying now?

My next 3 steps to obey what God has said:

Gratitude

What did God do for me last week?

What am I believing God for this week?

I will show my gratitude to the Lord by:

Reflections of Intimacy

Notes

Reflections of Intimacy

Notes

Notes

Reflections
of
Intimacy

Notes

Reflections
of
Intimacy

Notes

Notes

Notes